The]

2

Carl's view

I am aged 26.

I am going for a new job
this week.

I have an interview.

The interview is on
Thursday morning.

I'm a bit nervous about it.

The job is Assistant Store Manager.

The store is a furniture and carpet store.

It is called Carter's.

It is an out-of-town store.

I have worked there for
eighteen months.

I am a salesman.

I usually work in the
furniture department.

Tony, the last Assistant, said I should apply for the job.

I got on well with him.

He's got the Assistant Manager's job at IKEA.

We both want to get on in business.

I don't want to be a salesman all my life.

If I don't get this job, I will be looking for others.

I don't think that Brian, the Store Manager, likes me very much.

Soon after I started here, I got into his bad books.

I lost my temper with a customer.

You get some really difficult people sometimes.

This one complained about everything.

She just wouldn't listen to anything I said.

There will be three people to interview us on Thursday.

I don't know who they are yet.

Brian, the Store Manager, will be one of them.

And I think the Chairman will be there.

I don't know who the third one will be.

London Borough of Newham			
90800101056162			
A & H			
ABS	£8.50 per set		
NHSS	5353340		

5353340

The Interview series

1. The Manager's view
2. Carl's view
3. Leela's view
4. Gordon's view
5. Martin's view
6. Doreen's view

*

The Interview : Exercises
(Photocopy Master)

Brown and Brown

The Interview 2. Carl's view
ISBN 1 870596 87 0

ABS

The Interview

1

The Manager's view

Publishers: Brown and Brown,
             Keeper's Cottage,
             Westward,
             Wigton,
             Cumbria CA7 8NQ
             Tel. 016973 42915

First published 2002

ISBN 1 870596 86 2

Printed by Reed's Ltd., Penrith, Cumbria
on 100% recycled paper and card.